REBUILDING A REAL ECONOMY

Unleashing Engineering Innovation

SUMMARY OF A FORUM

Prepared by Steve Olson
for the
NATIONAL ACADEMY OF ENGINEERING
OF THE NATIONAL ACADEMIES

THE NATIONAL ACADEMIES PRESS
Washington, D.C.
www.nap.edu

THE NATIONAL ACADEMIES PRESS   500 Fifth Street, N.W.   Washington, DC 20001

NOTICE: The subject of this report is the forum held during the 2009 Annual Meeting of the National Academy of Engineering.

Opinions, finding, and conclusions expressed in this publication are those of the forum participants and not necessarily the views of the National Academy of Engineering.

International Standard Book Number-13: 978-0-309-15007-1
International Standard Book Number-10: 0-309-15007-8

Copies of this report are available from the National Academies Press, 500 Fifth Street, N.W., Lockbox 285, Washington, DC 20055; (888) 624-8373 or (202) 334-3313 (in the Washington metropolitan area); online at *http://www.nap.edu*.

For more information about the National Academy of Engineering, visit the NAE home page at **www.nae.edu**.

Copyright 2010 by the National Academies. All rights reserved.

Printed in the United States of America

THE NATIONAL ACADEMIES
Advisers to the Nation on Science, Engineering, and Medicine

The **National Academy of Sciences** is a private, nonprofit, self-perpetuating society of distinguished scholars engaged in scientific and engineering research, dedicated to the furtherance of science and technology and to their use for the general welfare. Upon the authority of the charter granted to it by the Congress in 1863, the Academy has a mandate that requires it to advise the federal government on scientific and technical matters. Dr. Ralph J. Cicerone is president of the National Academy of Sciences.

The **National Academy of Engineering** was established in 1964, under the charter of the National Academy of Sciences, as a parallel organization of outstanding engineers. It is autonomous in its administration and in the selection of its members, sharing with the National Academy of Sciences the responsibility for advising the federal government. The National Academy of Engineering also sponsors engineering programs aimed at meeting national needs, encourages education and research, and recognizes the superior achievements of engineers. Dr. Charles M. Vest is president of the National Academy of Engineering.

The **Institute of Medicine** was established in 1970 by the National Academy of Sciences to secure the services of eminent members of appropriate professions in the examination of policy matters pertaining to the health of the public. The Institute acts under the responsibility given to the National Academy of Sciences by its congressional charter to be an adviser to the federal government and, upon its own initiative, to identify issues of medical care, research, and education. Dr. Harvey V. Fineberg is president of the Institute of Medicine.

The **National Research Council** was organized by the National Academy of Sciences in 1916 to associate the broad community of science and technology with the Academy's purposes of furthering knowledge and advising the federal government. Functioning in accordance with general policies determined by the Academy, the Council has become the principal operating agency of both the National Academy of Sciences and the National Academy of Engineering in providing services to the government, the public, and the scientific and engineering communities. The Council is administered jointly by both Academies and the Institute of Medicine. Dr. Ralph J. Cicerone and Dr. Charles M. Vest are chair and vice chair, respectively, of the National Research Council.

www.national-academies.org

Preface

The financial crisis that began in 2008 is a stark demonstration that we as a nation take great risks when we build too much of our economy on a base that does not create real value. Relying on vaporous transactions to generate wealth is no substitute for making real products and providing real services. In the 21st century, the United States and the rest of the world will face some of the greatest challenges of the modern age: feeding a growing population, generating adequate energy without destroying the environment, countering chronic and emerging infectious diseases. The first decade of the new century has shown that technological innovation is essential for the United States and other countries to meet these challenges.

At the 2009 Annual Meeting of the National Academy of Engineering in Irvine, California, a public forum entitled "Rebuilding a Real Economy: Unleashing Engineering Innovation" brought together seven prominent leaders of the innovation system to discuss the challenges facing America. Jean-Lou Chameau, president of the California Institute of Technology, described how research universities can foster not only the new ideas at the heart of innovation but also the translation of those ideas into new products and services. Peter Diamandis, chairman and CEO of the X PRIZE Foundation, explained how large prizes can catalyze innovation to solve outstanding technological challenges. Judy Estrin, former chief technology officer of Cisco, emphasized the twin needs for taking risks and thinking long term. Chad Holliday, former chairman and CEO of DuPont, pointed out very real competitive threats facing our nation and suggested how we could counter those threats. Steve Koonin, under secretary of science at the Department of Energy, described necessary steps to provide the United States with secure and sustainable sources

NAE President Charles M. Vest introducing the forum participants. Photo by Tom Sullivan.

of energy. Raymond Lane, managing partner of Kleiner Perkins Caufield and Byers, laid out actions the government can take to promote innovation in the renewable energy sector. And Tony Tan Keng Yam, chairman of the National Research Foundation of Singapore, executive director of the Government of Singapore Investment Corporation, and former deputy prime minister of Singapore, offered an international perspective on the U.S. prospects in the global economy. The insights of the panel members cut to the heart of what this nation needs to do to remain a global leader in the turbulent world of the 21st century.

The forum was hosted by Ali Velshi, the chief business correspondent for CNN and host of the program "Your Money." Engaging a reporter to lead the discussion was a departure for the National Academy of Engineering, and it was extremely successful. Velshi has an extensive background in topics related to the economy and valuable firsthand experience in talking with people throughout the country about their concerns and hopes. His participation in the forum made for a lively and productive discussion.

This summary, which was written by Steve Olson, captures the main points made by the forum participants with the aim of encouraging further reflection and discussion.

As the panelists pointed out, no single action can reenergize our innovation system. A portfolio of interconnected and interdependent initiatives must be undertaken to generate new knowledge and technology and move that new knowledge successfully into a competitive world marketplace. But the panelists clarified the goal toward which we must strive and some of the most important steps we need to take to achieve that goal.

> Charles M. Vest
> President, National Academy of Engineering

Contents

1 The Ongoing Crisis — 1

2 Key Innovation Sectors — 7
    Research Universities, 7
    Entrepreneurs, 8
    National Laboratories, 10
    Manufacturing, 11

3 Policy Initiatives — 15
    Energy Policy, 15
    Incentive Prizes, 18
    The Example of Singapore, 20
    Education, 22

4 Prospects — 25

APPENDIXES

A Forum Agenda — 27
B Panelists' Biographies — 29

The Ongoing Crisis

Americans feel prosperous based largely on the performance of three key economic indicators, said Ali Velshi, chief business correspondent for CNN. Are the values of their homes rising faster than inflation? Are their investments, whether for their children's education or their own retirement, growing? And do their incomes equal or exceed increases in the cost of living?

In recent months, two of the three indicators have shown signs of improvement after declining precipitously during the financial crisis that began in 2008. Home prices have started to stabilize, though not everywhere and usually at levels below their previous highs. The stock market, which has gone up after reaching a low point early in 2009, has helped pull up other investments as well.

However, incomes have not been increasing across the board, Velshi noted. Furthermore, unemployment remains distressingly high, especially for particular groups, such as high school dropouts and manufacturing workers. "A manufacturing worker in some places in Indiana or Illinois or Ohio is simply not looking for another manufacturing job, because they're quite clear that [the jobs] are not there."

The economic pain of a high unemployment rate is compounded by profound uncertainty about the future direction of the U.S. economy. Policy makers talk about businesses that could make products and provide services for alternative sources of energy. But no one knows exactly what these industries will be or how many Americans they could employ. "We do not know what people who have been displaced are actually going to do in the next five to ten years," said Velshi. "We don't even know enough to tell them that perhaps they should move to different areas or retrain in certain industries. And

Ali Velshi, chief business correspondent for CNN and forum moderator. Photo by Tom Sullivan.

even if we did want to retrain them, we don't actually have a system by which we do that."

Peter Diamandis, chairman and CEO of the X PRIZE Foundation, agreed that the United States has seen the collapse of key industries, especially in manufacturing. But he added that in recent years we also have seen the "seemingly overnight creation of billion-dollar industries." He pointed to seven technology areas that are now or soon will be in periods of exponential growth: artificial intelligence, robotics, nanotechnology, ubiquitous computing networks, medicine and the human-machine interface, biotechnology and bioinformatics, and alternative energy and production systems. The important question, Diamandis said, is where these technologies will be developed and commercialized. As a historical example, he cited the contrasting experiences of St. Louis and Chicago. In 1904, when St. Louis hosted a world's fair, it was the fourth largest city in the United States, largely because it was on the Mississippi River and at the center of the riverboat industry. But as railroads began to take business away from steamboats, St. Louis did not embrace the new technology to the extent that Chicago did. Today,

Chicago is the third largest city in the United States and St. Louis is 52nd. It matters a great deal which technologies "a government bets on," Diamandis said.

Ultimately, economic prosperity and national security come from the blossoming of industries that drive massive efficiencies in education, knowledge creation, energy, and the production of goods, according to Diamandis. The economic boom of the 1990s can be traced in part to brilliant young entrepreneurs who initiated the dot-com revolution. The economic boom of the next two decades will originate with entrepreneurs who recognize and embrace the technologies of the future. Yet embracing these technologies can involve a "vicious struggle" between letting go of the past and siding with the new. The nation may need to let go of "labor-intensive [industries], capital-intensive industries, old-tech manufacturing, coal, oil, perhaps portions of agriculture—in other words, let go of the riverboat industries," Diamandis said. Instead, the public will have to be introduced to and reeducated in new paradigms and new industries that will redefine societies and determine standards of living for decades ahead.

> The economic boom of the next two decades will originate with entrepreneurs who recognize and embrace the technologies of the future.
>
> *Peter Diamandis*

Other countries are well aware of the potential of new technologies and will pose daunting competition to the United States. Chad Holliday, former chairman and CEO of DuPont, described a dinner in Shanghai at which he met the city's vice mayor for research and development. Holliday assumed that her job was oriented toward attracting businesses to the city, but she told him that she was in charge of four world-class laboratories. Astonished, he toured the laboratories the next day. "At seven in the morning we were touring her genomics laboratory, and it had exactly the same world-class equipment [as at DuPont], and every piece of equipment was being used." That is the competition for the United States, he said. Other countries are not just talking about competitiveness, "they're actually taking steps."

Holliday also recounted his experiences as a leader of the Council on Competitiveness, a nonpartisan and nongovernmental group of CEOs, university presidents, and labor leaders that has been working for more than two decades to improve the nation's long-term economic competitiveness. In recent years, other countries have been setting up similar organizations and have been looking to the U.S. council for guidance and inspiration. The week before the forum, the council organized a meeting of representatives of comparable organizations around the world who described a very large number of initiatives being taken in other countries to boost competitiveness. For example, the representative from Korea told Holliday that the corporate income tax rate for research-intensive companies in Korea is effectively zero because of the R&D tax credit. "They have taken this recession [as an opportunity,] not to talk about it, not to debate it, but to actually take steps. . . . We must do exactly the same thing."

Finally, Holliday described his experience at DuPont in building a very large manufacturing plant focused on solar technology. In looking for a country in which to build the plant—which features an area of clean space the size of six football fields—both Singapore and a partnership between China and Hong Kong immediately approached the company with very strong proposals. In the United States, said Holliday, he would not know whom to ask for help in soliciting such a proposal. Furthermore, when DuPont decided to accept the offer from China and Hong Kong but considered downsizing the plant because of the recent recession, the two countries offered to buy the output of the plant for the first several years at global market prices.

Several panelists discussed whether the recession that began in 2008 has been different from past recessions. Holliday insisted that the recession has been different "because in six weeks the total world collapsed together." The tight links between supply chains and information chains caused the slowdown to spread rapidly among markets and countries, he said. Furthermore, other countries are using the recession in new ways to shift the competitive balance among nations. "What we see going on in China and India and in a lot of other places is that they want to gain competitive position" as the economy recovers, but the United States today is not responding adequately to the ways globalization has changed the competitive challenge.

Judy Estrin, former CTO of Cisco and author of the book *Closing the Innovation Gap: Reigniting the Spark of Creativity in a Global Economy*, agreed that the world economy has become so interconnected, in part through the growth of the Internet, that the time frame in which people think about and react to new developments has shrunk considerably. This level of interconnectivity has both positive and negative consequences. The United States has traditionally been the world leader in building new industries based on innovation. "If we keep saying, 'It's the same, the system works, we just need to get back to normal,' we will

Tony Tan, chairman, National Research Foundation of Singapore, executive director, Government of Singapore Investment Corporation, and former deputy prime minister of Singapore. Photo by Tom Sullivan.

sabotage ourselves," she says. "What is providing great opportunities also creates unintended consequences that I don't think we as a country are aware enough of. We need to understand those consequences and take action to stem them."

Tony Tan Keng Yam, chairman of the National Research Foundation of Singapore, executive director, Government of Singapore Investment Corporation, and former deputy prime minister of Singapore, placed the challenges facing the United States in a global context. Many countries, including Singapore, have invested heavily in the economy of the United States because of its track record of innovation and growth. But Tan worries that the United States may react to the recession by erecting trade barriers and closing its borders to the influx of talented people from elsewhere in the world. He also cited the declining attention U.S. companies are giving to investments in R&D. "So many of the great inventions in the past in the U.S. came from labs like IBM and Bell Labs and so on. They are all disappearing, and we are left with fewer and fewer corporations that devote large amounts of their revenue to R&D." If companies do not invest in developing new ideas and new inventions, they will become uncompetitive. Yet U.S. companies have become so focused on achieving short-term results that they are putting fewer resources into endeavors that may have only long-term payoffs. "The financial community is so unforgiving of one bad year that corporations, management, [and] boards of directors do not feel that they have the capability of putting money into endeavors that will take several years before you see any results."

Key Innovation Sectors

The innovation system in the United States is like an ecosystem, said Estrin, with different sectors serving particular functions in close cooperation with other sectors. To meet the competitiveness challenges now facing the United States, the individual sectors and the relationships among sectors must both change.

RESEARCH UNIVERSITIES

Universities play a major role in the U.S. innovation system, said Jean-Lou Chameau, president of the California Institute of Technology. For example, many studies have documented the influence of university faculty members in commercializing intellectual property, both directly and indirectly. Start-up companies created by university faculty have a higher percentage of success than start-ups that originate in other institutions. "We need to keep reinforcing the links between faculty and the corporate world," Chameau said.

To enhance the benefits of university research, institutions of higher education need to embrace and support activities that merge academic disciplines. Some universities have taken steps in this direction, but much more needs to be done. The job of universities, said Chameau, must be "to create the physical, financial, and intellectual context for this merging to take place." An example would be linking and implementing knowledge across very different physical scales, from biotechnology, nanotechnology, and information technology to large-scale systems, such as energy, the physical infrastructure, and the environment. In the area of infrastructure, for instance, scientists will develop novel materials for infrastructure systems, but much more needs to be known about how the components of the systems function together.

Research universities also need to do much more to shape the public understanding of science, technology, and engineering. Science advisor John Holdren has suggested that scientists and engineers devote 10 percent of their time to such activities. "I'm not suggesting that, but we need to do better," said Chameau. It also is important for scientists and engineers not just to describe problems but to focus on potential solutions.

As with other parts of the innovation system, research universities are finding it harder to support highly risky undertakings. Universities and governments must work together to support high-risk research, not just research aimed at incremental advances. Some faculty members have been seeking funds from private foundations to do high-risk research, but this source of support is limited.

One policy innovation that could encourage the commercialization of ideas developed at research universities is for universities to provide more support for what Chameau called "vertical specialization." Institutions that can enhance the movement of early-stage technologies from laboratories and start-up companies to development by larger firms could be extremely beneficial in many industrial sectors. "This fits very well with what universities can do, and we're going to see more of that."

> Universities and governments must work together to support high-risk research, not just research aimed at incremental advances.
>
> Jean-Lou Chameau

ENTREPRENEURS

The United States has traditionally had a very strong entrepreneurial sector that has driven the development of new companies and new industries. But several factors have recently limited the productivity of this sector in the United States.

The major problem, said Estrin, is that the venture capital system "is broken." As venture capital funds have gotten bigger and become more accustomed to short-term returns, the number of firms willing to invest in high-risk, high-return ideas has decreased. In addition, the recession has reduced the number of angel investors, and the market for initial public offerings has significantly changed. Estrin urged that the venture capital industry become more like it was in the 1980s, when firms were more willing to take intelligent risks.

Raymond Lane, managing partner with the venture capital firm of Kleiner Perkins Caufield and Byers, agreed with Estrin's assessment. He said that too much venture capital is now available. If the venture capital market were more efficient, the available venture capital "would find the right entrepreneurs, and the cream would rise to the top." His firm looks at roughly 3,000 proposals a year to fund maybe 20 companies. "That's a lot of frogs to kiss to get those plans," Lane said. Also, many current venture capitalists do not have the experience of running companies, which reduces their ability to make good choices.

> The venture capital system is broken. As venture capital funds have gotten bigger and [investors] become more accustomed to short-term returns, the number of firms willing to invest in high-risk, high-return ideas has decreased.
>
> *Judy Estrin*

Several panelists mentioned the legal climate as a barrier to entrepreneurs. The potential for litigation "is a fundamental problem," said Diamandis. "We are becoming risk averse in this nation for a reason. If you are a large corporation and you take a large risk and you fail, you get hit with your stock price plummeting or lawsuits. If you are a government agency and you take risks, all of a sudden you have a congressional investigation. And without the ability to take risk, we are stuck at the status quo or at best incrementalism." Holliday agreed that legal requirements can be a major factor in business decisions. When DuPont agreed to build its solar plant in China, in 60 days it had every permit it needed to build and operate the plant. "In this country, if I could do it in 12 months, I'd have a celebration."

Policies that address the needs of the entrepreneurial sector could boost the conversion of innovations into jobs and economic growth. Entrepreneurs need more than the short-term stimulus afforded by the American Recovery and Reinvestment Act to enhance long-term returns, said Diamandis. New policies, such as R&D tax credits, could provide a more extended lift. Entrepreneurs also need to be featured in society so that young people want to emulate them. "In society today, especially in America, our heroes are the television stars, the sport stars, and [similar] individuals, which is unfortunate, because the real stars need to be the scientists, the engineers, the entrepreneurs. How do we focus our spotlight on these people?"

Holliday described a program undertaken by the Council on Competitiveness to enhance the climate for entrepreneurs at a regional level. So far the program has targeted seven regions of the country. In Wilmington, Delaware, for example, a survey of entrepreneurs found that news coverage of entrepreneurial activities was severely limited. An effort to provide information to newspapers has generated much more public attention. Similarly, a clearinghouse for entrepreneurs to learn about sources of venture capital has provided a way to connect innovators with potential funders. In addition, a program that brought together university presidents in the area provided a way for entrepreneurs to tap into expertise at local universities.

NATIONAL LABORATORIES

Laboratories supported by the federal government—including the large national laboratories funded by the Department of Energy—are unique American assets, said Steve Koonin, under secretary of science at the Department of Energy. They can conduct research, development, and demonstration projects that are not well suited to universities while also constructing and operating major facilities that are open to all researchers. More generally, they can serve as a bridge between research and commercialization to accelerate innovation.

Universities, national laboratories, the private sector, and government all have different roles, said Koonin. Universities provide new basic knowledge and train tomorrow's researchers and citizens. The private sector exists to make money, with start-up companies pursuing high-risk innovation and large corporations focused on taking new ideas to scale. The government establishes a policy environment and shapes the overall economy. Coordinating the activities of these different sectors can be difficult. Universities shy away from significant commercial involvement, and ownership of intellectual property is often a source of tension. Businesses must seek differential advantage if they are to be successful, while government seeks to provide a level playing field for companies. "In sum, all of the players have current conceptions of their roles that are hard to change

> "In sum, all of the players have current conceptions of their roles that are hard to change but indeed must change if [innovation] is to proceed at the pace to which we aspire."
>
> Jean-Lou Chameau

but indeed must change if [innovation] is to proceed at the pace to which we aspire."

In some ways, the national laboratories provide a research environment similar to that created at some of the large industrial laboratories of the past, such as Bell Laboratories or the laboratories supported by IBM. Partnerships between national laboratories and other institutions also provide a way to couple different parts of the innovation system. For example, Chameau described an ongoing partnership among NASA, the Jet Propulsion Laboratory, and Caltech that has been a great success.

MANUFACTURING

The United States has many strengths in the areas of invention, innovation, and early-stage research and development, said Koonin. But it has been less strong in the deployment of innovations into high-value-added manufacturing.

Holliday noted that incentives and policies in place today in the United States discourage companies from locating manufacturing jobs in this country. For example, the technologies deployed in the solar plant DuPont built in China were developed in the United States, but most of the jobs ended up in China. The United States needs "to attract not just the technology development here but the jobs here."

> Incentives and policies in place today in the United States discourage companies from locating manufacturing jobs in this country.
>
> *Chad Holliday*

Koonin observed that federal agencies play an important role in boosting manufacturing in the United States. But the focal point for this issue is Capitol Hill, and legislators "need to get more focused on this issue than they have."

Diamandis asked whether government investments in U.S. manufacturing are properly targeted. He pointed out that the federal government is spending on the order of $130 billion bailing out the automobile industry, representing an average of $200,000 per worker in the industry. "What if we spent that money retooling and reeducating those individuals, keeping them employed but for other industries that are critical to our needs, such as energy production and installation, battery power, solar, whatever? We have to make some tough decisions about what industries—the riverboats versus the railroads—that we want to be in over the next ten years. And it's going to hurt."

Judy Estrin, author and serial entrepreneur. Photo by Tom Sullivan.

Americans can still manufacture products at lower costs than the global competition, said Lane. But to do so they need to take advantage of new production systems that greatly improve efficiency. "If we think in old ways and say, 'We're going to build cars or any product the way we did 20 years ago,' we lose, because our cost per hour is higher. But if we can use less labor and create higher-value manufacturing jobs, we win."

In this regard, Holliday pointed to agriculture in the United States as an example of an industrial sector that has become a world leader by adopting modern technologies and production systems.

Looking at the U.S. economy as a whole, Estrin noted that there is a fine balance between competitiveness and globalization. Too strong a focus on competitiveness can lead to protectionism. But innovation can produce lots of winners, not just one. The United States must "partner within a global environment to solve the challenges that face us as a nation and a planet."

> Looking at the U.S. economy as a whole, there is a fine balance between competitiveness and globalization. Too strong a focus on competitiveness can lead to protectionism.
>
> Judy Estrin

However, the United States cannot be a partner from a position of weakness, Estrin continued. The best collaborations occur when each partner feels strong. Lane agreed that new industries can produce many winners. "But I, for one, am for globalization if American companies that build American jobs win, first, and global companies that build American jobs win, second, and globalization for the good of mankind, third." Thirty years ago the number one concern of Americans was peace, he said. "Today it is jobs, jobs, jobs."

Policy Initiatives

ENERGY POLICY

The use of energy is deeply embedded in the economy and society of the United States. The country spends about a trillion dollars a year on energy, according to Lane, and another trillion dollars on devices that use energy. "It is a big business, possibly the biggest."

The United States is currently locked in a competitive battle with other countries for leadership in the energy business of the 21st century. Over the next five years, said Lane, the United States will be making decisions that will determine its world standing in the energy industry, and those decisions will have effects lasting for decades.

The United States is clearly not winning the competition today. At present, our policy, as Al Gore has put it, is to borrow money from China, buy oil from the Middle East, and burn it here. China, meanwhile, understands that it must control its energy future and that the future will not be the same as the past. Government policies in China have established fuel economy standards for vehicles that are well above standards in the United States. By 2020, China is slated to be generating five times as much wind energy as the United States, creating 120,000 jobs in that country.

> Over the next five years the United States will be making decisions that will determine its world standing in the energy industry.
>
> *Ray Lane*

The largest Internet companies today, including Amazon, E-Bay, Microsoft, and Yahoo, were all created in the United States, Lane pointed out. But of the world's largest wind energy companies, only one, General Electric, is an American company. The United States has just one of the

Wind farm in Palm Springs, California.

top ten solar companies in the world, one of the world's top ten wind turbine companies, and two of the top ten advanced battery companies. The United States "led the development of not only the steel industry and other industries in the 1900s but [also] the electronics industry, the biotech industry, and the Internet. In clean energy, we are clearly behind the rest of the world."

Innovation is the way to catch up, said Lane. His company has funded approximately 50 energy companies based on high-risk ideas. "I'm not in the subprime business, I'm in the sub-subprime business, because we loan money to people who have taken the ultimate risk."

Lane listed five ways government could boost the competitiveness of the U.S. energy industry. First, government should establish a long-term price on carbon and cap carbon dioxide emissions worldwide. Without this price signal, it is difficult for private industry to know how the market is going to react or when an economic return will be possible. Second, new policies should be adapted to encourage utilities to drive efficiency, develop and use renewable sources of energy, and build a standardized, unified, smart electricity grid.

Third, stricter fuel economy standards for cars should be adopted. "Let's get aggressive. We don't have to sit with the [standards] that have been adopted." Fourth, R&D on energy production, distribution, storage, and use should be increased. Even with the increases promoted by the Obama administration, energy R&D is still just a quarter of one percent of the national energy bill.

Fifth, the government should change trade laws so that the United States becomes a leading exporter of energy technologies. "The Chinese should be buying our technology, not us buying their technology," Lane said. Negotiations on reducing worldwide emissions "must be looked at as a commercial opportunity for us to lead global industries."

Koonin agreed that "many energy technologies developed in the U.S. are now dominated by other countries," including photovoltaics, automobile efficiency, batteries, electricity transmission, power electronics, and nuclear power. Furthermore, because the energy infrastructure is so longlasting, competitive advantages can be locked into place for long periods. Unlike electronic technologies, such as personal audio and video, the energy system changes on a decadal timescale. "Power plants last 50 years. Automobiles last 15 years. There is also the ubiquity of energy, meaning that many people have interests in it, and those interests don't always align." Finally, the current energy system offers good ways of producing heat, light, and mobility, "so new technologies have to meet those benchmarks of cost and availability if they are to be successful."

> Negotiations on reducing worldwide emissions "must be looked at as a commercial opportunity for us to lead global industries."
>
> *Ray Lane*

Koonin reiterated the need for many of the policies advocated by Lane, including significant and consistent carbon prices, renewable or low-carbon power portfolio standards, efficiency standards, energy R&D, and the development of human capital. He noted that the Department of Energy is pursuing a variety of programs to stimulate energy innovation. Energy frontier research centers are focused on basic science and technology. The Advanced Research Projects Agency-Energy (ARPA-E) has begun to fund high-risk, high-reward concepts. Stimulus funds and ongoing support are being applied to innovation in vehicle technologies and manufacturing, carbon capture and storage, renewables, and grid modernization. "We are making tangible progress toward making a difference in energy innovation."

It is important to move quickly, said Koonin, because "the atmosphere is filling up with carbon dioxide." The levels of carbon dioxide projected for the middle of this century under a business as usual model will endanger the climate. Yet the infrastructure that is being built today will still be functioning 50 years from now. Many steps can be taken immediately that would have long-term positive effects, such as improving the efficiency of the internal combustion engine, gradual electrification of the automobile fleet from hybrids to plug-in hybrids to full batteries, development of advanced biofuels, greater efficiency of energy use, nuclear power, wind power, carbon capture and storage, and building efficiency.

> "To capture the jobs stemming from energy innovation, we have to reverse the U.S. decline in manufacturing and make the country again a favored venue for production."
>
> Steven Koonin

An additional challenge in the energy industry is to generate jobs in the United States rather than in other countries. "To capture the jobs stemming from energy innovation, we have to reverse the U.S. decline in manufacturing and make the country again a favored venue for production," Koonin said. Doing so requires addressing many nontechnical issues that are outside the scope of the Energy Department, such as labor costs, health care, and tax regimes. "Without addressing those, the U.S. will not realize the full benefits of our technical achievements."

INCENTIVE PRIZES

Diamandis described an innovative approach to driving innovation: offering large monetary prizes for clearly defined technological achievements. The X PRIZE Foundation that he heads develops prizes in four broad areas: energy and the environment, exploration, education and global development, and the life sciences. "Humans love a challenge," said Diamandis. "We are genetically evolved to compete. That's what we do best, in our sports, in our lives, whatever it might be. We do our best thinking in a race, whether it's to build the atom bomb, to get to the Moon, or to build private spaceships."

The approach taken by the foundation has a number of benefits, Diamandis said. If prizes are structured properly, they can generate 10 to 40 times the amount of the prize money in investments. They also are very efficient, because "you only pay the winner." They attract small,

POLICY INITIATIVES

Peter Diamandis, chairman and CEO, X Prize Foundation. Photo by Tom Sullivan.

young, and sometimes naive teams, many of which include mavericks who bring new ways of thinking to a field. They encourage risk taking and bring new sources of capital to important problems, including problems in industries that are in need of revitalization. Ultimately, they can change what people think is possible, "because if you think something is impossible, it is," Diamandis said.

The Ansari X PRIZE is an excellent example. It offered a $10 million prize to the first private team to build and launch a spacecraft capable of carrying three people to an altitude of 100 kilometers twice within two weeks. The prize was won on October 4, 2004, after generating expenditures of $100 million by 26 teams from seven nations. Another example is a prize offered by the Defense Advanced Research Projects Agency (DARPA). For 20 years people had spent hundreds of millions of dollars trying to develop an autonomous vehicle, but little progress was made.

> "We are genetically evolved to compete. That's what we do best, in our sports, in our lives, whatever it might be. We do our best thinking in a race, whether it's to build the atom bomb, to get to the Moon, or to build private spaceships."
>
> *Peter Diamandis*

When DARPA established a $2 million prize for an autonomous car, a team of graduate students at Stanford University built one in less than a year for half a million dollars. Diamandis continued:

> That, for me, is the vibrancy and excitement that we need to be generating. The day before something is a breakthrough, it's a crazy idea. If it weren't a crazy idea, it wouldn't be a breakthrough; it would be an incremental improvement. So where in our large corporations and our government agencies do we embrace and allow for crazy ideas to materialize? Where do we fund, tolerate, and encourage failure, and not only failure but serial failure? Breakthroughs require a great deal of risk and a tolerance for risk. Worse yet, true innovations are often a radical departure from accepted theories, modes of business, and beliefs and as such are heretical to the experts until ultimately they are proven true. So how do we ultimately balance the desire for breakthroughs with the inherent institutional inertia of large corporations and governments?

THE EXAMPLE OF SINGAPORE

Changing the production system of a country in relatively short order is far from impossible, said Tony Tan Keng Yam, chairman of the National Research Foundation and former deputy prime minister of Singapore. In fact, Singapore has transformed its economy several times since gaining independence from Great Britain in 1965. First it transitioned from labor-intensive industries to skill-intensive industries. Then the country moved into technology-intensive industries. And currently it is pursuing knowledge-based, innovation-driven industries. "Transforming our economy has been a way of life in Singapore," said Tan.

In the process, Singapore has greatly increased the incomes of its citizens. Desperately poor upon independence, the country now has the second highest per capita income in Asia after Japan. The achievement is even more remarkable given that Singapore, a small country of just 5 million people living on 700 square kilometers, has no natural resources and imports all of its food and half of its water.

> The key to Singapore's success has been its ability to anticipate future developments and to take risks.
>
> Tony Tan

The key to Singapore's success has been its ability to anticipate future developments and to take risks. When the country became independent, the conventional wisdom was to erect trade barriers to protect local industries. Instead, Singapore lowered trade barriers, and today it is host to almost 7,000 companies from the United States,

Singapore harbor.

Europe, and Japan, more than 3,000 companies from China and India, and more than 2,500 companies from Australia and New Zealand, Tan said.

A second example is that Singapore converted its port operations to emphasize container shipping at a time when the world marine industry was still debating whether containers were the future of shipping. Today Singapore's port is connected to more than 600 ports in more than 100 countries around the world and handles some 20 million containers annually.

Tan cited a third example, the water industry in Singapore. With few water resources, the country has invested heavily in water research, technology, and management since the 1970s. In the process, it has transformed an inherent resource constraint into a new economic growth sector as the world deals with the problem of supplying growing populations with adequate water. In 2007, Singapore's water industry won the Stockholm Industry Water Award.

The government of Singapore has shaped the continual transformation of industry through guidance and funding and by "providing a mechanism within the government for public officers to help them think out of the box and bring about new developments and new ways of delivering public service," said Tan. The government is in the process of raising its spending on R&D from under 2.5 percent of the country's gross domestic product to 3 percent. Every government ministry in Singapore devotes a percentage of its budget to innovation. In addition, the National Research Foundation of Singapore has created a campus for research excellence and technological enterprise that houses research centers established by world-class universities. In broad terms, Singapore has established a national framework for innovation and enterprise that integrates the chain of knowledge creation, knowledge diffusion, and knowledge use to create a vibrant innovation ecosystem.

Most important, said Tan, Singapore has emphasized the education of its citizens. "Education has always been given the highest priority in Singapore since our independence in 1965," said Tan. "Rightly so, because with no natural resources, our people are the only strength that Singapore has." The country has built technical institutes of education and research universities that can serve as engines of growth. It also has emphasized the translation of ideas and innovations from the university to the marketplace, which has helped generate new industries, new companies, and new business models.

> If you look at the history of discoveries in this country since World War II, it is always related to a relatively small number of individuals. We should not worry only about the numbers [of science and engineering students] but about identifying and nurturing those who can make a difference.
>
> Jean-Lou Chameau

EDUCATION

Education will be just as critical a determinant of the United States' future economic success as it has been in Singapore. To succeed in innovation, students must be trained to be innovators, said Chameau. In universities, faculty should support students' work on ideas that they initiate. "If you look at surveys of freshmen conducted every year, they love that approach," he said. "They want to develop a meaningful philosophy of life, they want to get engaged, and we need to find ways to do that." Students are particularly drawn to grand challenges, such as those awarded by the X PRIZE Foundation or those issued by the National Academy of Engineering in 2008.

Jean-Lou Chameau, president, California Institute of Technology. Photo by Tom Sullivan.

For innovation to become a more prominent feature of American society, science and technology must be more integrated into a liberal education. "Are graduates of history or philosophy well-rounded if, in the 21st century, they are limited in their knowledge of science and technology?" Chameau asked. "I think this is an important issue for the country." To achieve this goal, science and engineering faculty in universities will have to devote more time to teaching classes for non-specialists and revisiting curricula and courses.

Chameau cautioned against focusing too intently on the immediate needs of the marketplace. As a dean of engineering in the 1990s, he was under pressure to produce more software engineers and computer scientists, just as the rush today is for people to become energy scientists and technologists. "At the same time, we have to remember . . . to educate people who are going to be active over 20 or 30 years, to make sure that we pay attention to the fundamental disciplines. We don't really know what will be the next big thing."

Science and engineering faculty will also have to direct particular attention to the relatively small numbers of prospective scientists and engineers who will make a real difference in their fields. "If you look at the history of discoveries in this country since World War II, it is always related to a relatively small number of individuals," Chameau said. "We should not worry only about the numbers [of science and engineering students] but about identifying and nurturing those who can make a difference."

> "In today's world, success will come from having the largest possible educated population and providing those hundreds of millions of creative individuals with the freedom and the capital to create and be brilliant."
>
> *Peter Diamandis*

As Diamandis said, "For the leadership of modern nations, success will not come from having the largest defense industry. Nor the most natural resources. Nor even the most advanced technologies. In today's world, success will come from having the largest possible educated population and providing those hundreds of millions of creative individuals with the freedom and the capital to create and be brilliant."

Prospects

Despite the many challenges confronting the United States, the panelists were generally optimistic about the nation's prospects. Tan observed that from an outsider's perspective, the United States retains unique strengths. "Non-Americans are usually much more optimistic for America than Americans," he said. "People [in the United States] are more focused on short-term problems and forget the resilience and diversity and strength of American business and American society." Despite the difficult problems facing the United States, the country still represents the largest single destination of Singapore's investments. "There is no other country in the world with a depth of markets and a breadth of markets where you can deploy large sums of money."

The United States has another unique strength that no other country shares, said Tan—the ability to attract to its shores large numbers of the brightest people in the world. These talented and ambitious people work in universities and corporations and bring their skills and persistence to their adopted country. "I think that this is a key to American success over the centuries."

> The United States has a unique strength—the ability to attract large numbers of the brightest people in the world. . . . this is a key to American success. . . .
>
> *Tony Tan*

Many of the industries in which innovation and growth will be strongest can already be identified, said Estrin, particularly in energy science and technology, health care, and education. Many of the panelists were especially encouraged by rapid recent progress in the life sciences. The ability to sequence human genomes quickly and cheaply "is going to revolutionize medicine, making it preventative and predictive," said Diamandis. According to Koonin, the interface between biology and energy will be "incredibly fertile." The combination of chemistry with biotechnology will make it possible "to solve problems that we couldn't solve before," said Holliday. "There is no other country close to where we are today."

The U.S. government has demonstrated its ability to cope with major problems. The government gave out more than a trillion dollars in a short period to bail out floundering banks because the industry was failing. "The crisis we are talking about today is a more serious long-term crisis than the one we just dealt with," said Holliday. "Somehow we have to muster the attention."

> "Every challenge and every problem . . . we face on this planet can . . . be solved by the passionate and committed human mind."
>
> *Peter Diamandis*

One major challenge in capturing the attention of the government and voting public is to foster long-term rather than short-term perspectives. The stimulus funding was designed to have an immediate impact, whereas innovation may not create new jobs for several years. "But we have to start today, because if we keep waiting, we keep delaying that process," said Estrin. "We don't as a country think long term."

Many engineers were heavily influenced by the Apollo project, Diamandis pointed out, and the lessons of the Apollo project can still inspire the American public, just as they inspired him when he was a boy. "Every challenge and every problem that we face on this planet can in fact be solved by the passionate and committed human mind."

Appendix A

Forum Agenda

Annual Meeting Forum
Rebuilding a Real Economy: Unleashing Engineering Innovation

Monday, October 5, 2009
9:30 am – 12:30 pm, Pacific Time
Arnold and Mabel Beckman Center of The National Academies
University of California, Irvine

The Forum at the annual meeting on October 5, 2009, will bring the perspectives of experienced leaders of various sectors to the critical topic of unleashing engineering innovation in order to rebuild a real economy.

The United States is facing an economic crisis unmatched in recent memory. There is general consensus that this crisis was precipitated by building far too much of our economy on vaporous transactions that did not create real value.

To emerge from this financial crisis and set a sound 21st century course, we must turn our attention to unleashing technological innovation to create products and services that add actual value. As a nation we must refocus on the real economy, and that will require a reenergized innovation system to generate new knowledge and technology and move them successfully to the competitive world marketplace. We must become more productive and efficient at the things we already do well, create new industries, and transform others. We need to address energy, environment, security, and health care delivery in order to sustain our economic stability and quality of life. Our innovation system itself must evolve to meet these large-scale challenges.

President Obama recently noted that the horrendous loss of manufacturing jobs "underscores the importance of generating new businesses and industries to replace the ones we've lost, and of preparing our workers to fill the jobs they create." *Rising Above the Gathering Storm* defined the necessary federal investments and policy changes to enable this, the NAE *Engineering Grand Challenges* and the Academies' *America's Energy Future* set the stage, and now we must focus on execution.

The distinguished panel (see below) will explore the roles of academia, entrepreneurs, venture capitalists, global corporations, challenge prizes, and governments in unleashing technological innovation to rebuild a real economy and meet 21st century challenges. They will also share thoughts about what new broadly empowering technologies may develop to facilitate economic growth.

Moderator:

Ali Velshi, chief business correspondent and co-host of *Your Money*, CNN

Panel:

- Jean-Lou Chameau, president of Caltech and former provost of Georgia Tech
- Peter Diamandis, chairman and CEO of the X Prize Foundation
- Judy Estrin, former CTO of Cisco, serial entrepreneur, and author on innovation
- Chad Holliday, former chairman and CEO of DuPont
- Steve Koonin, U.S. Under Secretary of Energy for Science, former vice president of BP, and former provost of Caltech
- Raymond Lane, managing partner of Kleiner Perkins Caufield and Byers and former president of Oracle
- Tony Tan Keng Yam, former deputy prime minister of Singapore, now chairman of the National Research Foundation (of Singapore) and executive director of the Government of Singapore Investment Corporation

Appendix B

Panelists' Biographies

ALI VELSHI is chief business correspondent for CNN; host of *Your Money,* a weekend business roundtable; a regular contributor and anchor for *Issue #1*; and host of *The Ali Velshi Show*, a weekly call-in radio program on CNN Radio and *CNN.com Live*. In addition, "The Ali V Podcast" is available at *www.CNN.com/podcasting* and on iTunes.

A veteran of financial news, Velshi recently hosted *The Turnaround*, a show to promote small business, and was an anchor at *CNNfn*. Before joining *CNNfn* in 2001, he hosted *The Business News*, Canada's only prime-time business news hour. Earlier in his career, Velshi was business anchor for Cable Pulse 24 and its sister station, CITY TV and a reporter for CFTO-TV. In 1996, he was awarded a fellowship to the U.S. Congress by the American Political Sciences Association; during his fellowship he worked with U.S. Rep. Lee Hamilton (D-Ind.).

Born in Kenya and raised in Toronto, Velshi graduated from Queens University in Canada with a degree in religion. His first book, *Gimme My Money Back: Your Guide to Beating the Financial Crisis*, was released in January 2009.

JEAN-LOU CHAMEAU, former provost of Georgia Institute of Technology, became the eighth president of the California Institute of Technology (Caltech) in 2006. Committed to carrying on the institute's tradition of excellence in science and technology, Chameau has promoted a multi-disciplinary approach to research and education, encouraging the development of programs in energy, medical

science, and the environment. His focus has been on ensuring that students have meaningful and stimulating educational experiences, increasing diversity in the Caltech community, and increasing entrepreneurial opportunities for faculty and students. Chameau was elected to the National Academy of Engineering in 2009.

PETER DIAMANDIS is chairman and CEO of the X PRIZE Foundation (*www.xprize.org*), a nonprofit organization that offers large-incentive prizes to support radical breakthroughs in science and technology that will benefit humanity. Best known for the $10 million Ansari X PRIZE for private space flight, the foundation is launching prizes in four categories (energy and the environment, exploration, education and global development, and the life sciences) and has three active prizes—the $10 million Archon X PRIZE for Genomics, the $30 million Google Lunar X PRIZE, and the $10 million Progressive Automotive X PRIZE.

An international leader in the commercial space arena, Dr. Diamandis is cofounder and managing director of Space Adventures (*www.spaceadventures.com*), a company that has brokered the travel of private citizens to the International Space Station; co-founder and CEO of Zero Gravity Corporation (*www.gozerog.com*), a company that develops private, FAA-certified parabolic flight of a Boeing 727-200 aircraft; and chairman and co-founder of the Rocket Racing League (*www.rocketracingleague.com*).

In 2008, Dr. Diamandis cofounded Singularity University (*www.singularityU.org*), of which he is vice chancellor and chairman. In 1987, he co-founded and was the first managing director of the International Space University (*www.isunet.edu*). Prior to that, Diamandis was chairman of Students for the Exploration and Development of Space (SEDS), an organization he founded at Massachusetts Institute of Technology (MIT) in 1980.

Diamandis has received many honors and awards, going back to the eighth grade, when he won first place in a rocket design contest. His recent honors include: the 2007 Arthur C. Clarke Award for Innovation; 2006 (inaugural) Heinlein Award; 2006 Lindbergh Award; 2006 Wired RAVE Award; 2006 Neil Armstrong Award for Aerospace Achievement and Leadership; the Konstantine Tsiolkovsky Award; the Aviation & Space Technology Laurel (twice); and the 2003 World Technology Award for Space. His personal motto is: "The best way to predict the future is to create it yourself!"

Dr. Diamandis received his undergraduate degree in molecular genetics and his graduate degree in aerospace engineering from MIT. He then attended Harvard Medical School where he earned his M.D. In 2005, he was awarded an honorary doctorate from the International Space University.

JUDY ESTRIN is CEO of JLABS LLC (formerly Packet Design Management Company LLC) and author of *Closing the Innovation Gap* (McGraw-Hill, 2008). Beginning in 1981, Estrin co-founded three successful technology companies: Bridge Communications, Network Computing Devices, and Precept Software. In 1998, Cisco Systems acquired Precept, and she became Cisco's chief technology officer, a position she held until April 2000.

Ms. Estrin has been named three times to the *Fortune Magazine* list of the 50 most powerful women in American business. She is also a member of the boards of directors of The Walt Disney Company, FedEx Corporation, Packet Design Inc., and Arch Rock. She is also on the advisory councils of the Stanford School of Engineering and the Stanford Bio-X Initiative. Ms. Estrin has a B.S. in mathematics and computer science from UCLA and an M.S. in electrical engineering from Stanford University.

CHAD HOLLIDAY has been chairman of the board of DuPont since January 1, 1999, and was chief executive officer of DuPont from February 1, 1998, until his retirement on January 31, 2009. Only the 18th executive to lead the company, which has been in business for more than 200 years, Holliday introduced a new mission for the company—to increase shareholder and societal value while decreasing the company's environmental footprint and achieving sustainable growth.

A member of the National Academy of Engineering, Holliday is past chairman of the Business Roundtable Task Force for Environment, Technology and Economy; the World Business Council for Sustainable Development (WBCSD); The Business Council; and the Society of Chemical Industry-American Section. He is also on the board of directors of Deere & Co. and CH2M HILL and is Chair Emeritus of the board of directors of Catalyst, chairman of the U.S. Council on Competitiveness, and a founding member of the International Business Council. He is co-author (with Stephan

Schmidheiny and Philip Watts) of *Walking the Talk: The Business Case for Sustainable Development* (Berrett-Koehler Publishers, 2002), a book that presents the business case for sustainable development and corporate responsibility.

Mr. Holliday received a B.S. in industrial engineering from the University of Tennessee and is a licensed Professional Engineer.

STEVEN E. KOONIN, U.S. Under Secretary of Energy for Science, was chief scientist for BP p.l.c., where he was responsible for carrying out  the company's long-range technology strategy, particularly for alternative and renewable energy. Koonin joined BP in 2004 after a 29-year career as professor of theoretical physics and provost at the California Institute of Technology (Caltech). Dr. Koonin has served on numerous advisory bodies for the National Science Foundation, U.S. Department of Defense, and U.S. Department of Energy national laboratories. His research interests include theoretical and computational physics, as well as global environmental science.

Dr. Koonin did his undergraduate work at Caltech and has a Ph.D. from the Massachusetts Institute of Technology.

RAY LANE, managing partner at Kleiner Perkins Caufield & Byers (KPCB), focuses on helping entrepreneurs with technological and market insight, organizational development, team building, selling, and managing growth. Since joining KPCB, he has sponsored investments in companies that work on enterprise and consumer technology, as well as clean and alternative energy.

Before joining KPCB, Lane was president and chief operating officer of Oracle Corporation, the second-largest software company in the  world and the leading enterprise software and services company. During his eight-year tenure, Oracle underwent phenomenal growth in revenue (from approximately $1 billion in 1992 to more than $10 billion in 2000). Under his leadership, the company expanded its business beyond database technology into enterprise applications and professional services.

Before joining Oracle, Lane was a senior partner with Booz-Allen & Hamilton, where he pioneered and led the Information Systems Group, a worldwide consulting practice that helps senior management achieve better results from information technology. He also served on the company's board of directors and executive management committee. Prior to that, he was division vice president at Electronic Data Systems Corp. (EDS). In addition, he spent 10 years with IBM in various product-management, sales, and marketing positions.

Lane received a B.S. in mathematics and an honorary Ph.D. in science from West Virginia University (WVU) and was elected to the Academy of Distinguished Graduates of WVU, was a director of the WVU Foundation Board, and is currently on the WVU Board of Governors. The Lane Department of Computer Science and Electrical Engineering is named in his honor. Also a member (and current chair) of the board of trustees of Carnegie Mellon University, Lane has actively campaigned for the establishment of a Silicon Valley campus; he is also co-creator of a High Dependability Computing Consortium between Carnegie Mellon and NASA.

Lane is vice chairman of Special Olympics International and has served on the International Board of Special Olympics for several years. He also holds an honorary Ph.D. from Golden Gate University.

TONY TAN KENG YAM is chairman of the National Research Foundation (of Singapore), executive director of the Government of Singapore Investment Corporation, and former Deputy Prime Minister of Singapore. Tan was appointed minister for education in June 1980 and was concurrently vice-chancellor of the National University of Singapore. A year later, he was appointed minister for trade and industry. From October 1983 to January 1985, Dr. Tan was minister for finance and concurrently minister for trade and industry. From January 1985 to December 1991, he was the minister for education.

In December 1991, Dr. Tan returned to the private sector as chairman and chief executive officer of Oversea-Chinese Banking Corporation. He rejoined the government in August 1995 when he was appointed deputy prime minister and minister for defence. In August 2003, he was appointed deputy prime minister and coordinating minister for security and defence.

In September 2005, Dr. Tan left the Cabinet to become deputy chairman and executive director of the Government of Singapore Investment Corporation Private Limited, chairman of the National Research Foundation, deputy chairman of the Research, Innovation and Enterprise Council, and chairman of Singapore Press Holdings Limited.